LEARNING.
.... **services**

Cornwall College St Austell
Learning Centre – Zone

This resource is to be returned on or before the last date
stamped below. To renew items please contact the Centre

Three Week Loan

Raintree   www.raintreepublishers.co.uk

To order:
Phone 44 (0) 1865 888112
Send a fax to 44 (0) 1865 314091
Visit the Raintree bookshop at
www.raintreepublishers.co.uk
to browse our catalogue and order online.

Produced by
David West ♟ Children's Books
7 Princeton Court
55 Felsham Road
London SW15 1AZ

Picture Research: Carlotta Cooper
Designer: Gary Jeffrey
Editor: James Pickering

First published in Great Britain by
Raintree, Halley Court, Jordan Hill,
Oxford OX2 8EJ, part of Harcourt Education.
Raintree is a registered trademark of Harcourt
Education Ltd.

Printed and bound in Italy

ISBN 1 844 43088 X (hardback)
07 06 05 04 03
10 9 8 7 6 5 4 3 2 1

ISBN 1 844 43093 6 (paperback)
08 07 06 05 04
10 9 8 7 6 5 4 3 2 1

British Library Cataloguing in Publication Data
Job, Chris
BMX. – (Extreme sports)
796.6'2
A full catalogue record for this book is available
from the British Library.

Acknowledgements
The publishers would like to thank the following
for permission to reproduce photographs:

Abbreviations: t-top, m-middle, b-bottom, r-right,
l-left, c-centre.

Front cover - Corbis. Pages 3, 5r, 11t, m & b, 16-
17b, 17 all, 20-21, 23t & r, 24bl & br, 25tl & bl,
26l, 26-27t, 29tl & bl - Steve Jackson. 6l, 7 all, 8
all, 9m & b, 10tr, 12l, 13t, 14l, 14-15, 15l, 16-17t,
18, 18-19, 21t, 25br, 28 both - James Hudson. 6br
- The Kobal Collection/Universal. 10br, 12b, 12-13,
13b, 15tr, 16l, 22b, 29r - Buzz Pictures. 12, 30 -
Corbis Images. 27b - Damien Elliott/Dig Magazine.

Every effort has been made to contact copyright
holders of any material reproduced in this book.
Any omissions will be rectified in subsequent
printings if notice is given to the publishers.

*An explanation of difficult words can be
found in the glossary on page 31.*

extreme sports

BMX

Chris Job

Raintree

CONTENTS

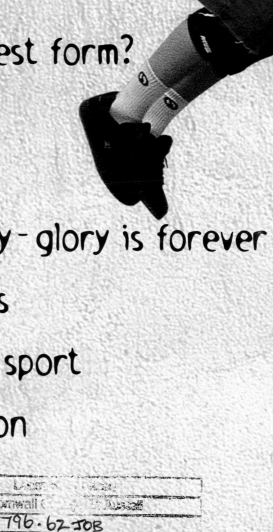

FLY LIKE A BIRD! Kicking his legs out behind him, James Hitchcox demonstrates a Superman jump. Some trick names are obvious, some a little less so!

Introduction

BMX has its roots in the Californian sunshine of the late 1960s. Early riders wanted to imitate motocross races on rough tracks. The term 'Bicycle Motocross' was coined, or BMX for short. Many BMX styles developed in a very short period of time. Riders might consider themselves to be a ramp rider, a dirt jumper, a flatlander, a street rider, or a racer. However different these disciplines might be, they all share the same roots, which can be summed up in three simple letters – BMX.

4 METRES OF AIR
A vertical height pole proves that Simon Tabron can leap, or 'air' a full 4 metres (13 feet) above a ramp.

WARNING!
BMX CAN BE AN **EXTREMELY DANGEROUS** SPORT. DO NOT ATTEMPT ANY MOVES **BEYOND YOUR ABILITIES** AND ALWAYS WEAR THE APPROPRIATE SAFETY EQUIPMENT.

The 1970s and 1980s

Racing in the early 1970s was a chaotic business. Often, twelve or more riders competed at the same time. Bikes were often difficult to control, with heavy frames and plastic mud guards. Few people realized that less weight meant more speed.

Racing grows up

Events such as the Yamaha Gold Cup, at the LA Coliseum in 1975, began to expose BMX racing to the American public. The race scene really took off in the late 1970s and early 1980s. The bikes became easier to ride, lighter and stronger. Often, as many as 2000 riders turned up to compete at national races.

UNIFORM
Full leathers were the standard uniform for racing.

HEAD TO HEAD
The format of BMX racing has remained largely unchanged over the years – eight riders go head to head out of the gate.

A BMX for Christmas

The film *E.T.* was released in 1982, and BMX played a large part throughout. It seemed that everyone bought a BMX bike after that. Like all fads, the trend for BMX didn't last forever. But this era produced a generation of riders who went on to shape the future of the sport.

MASS MEDIA!
E.T. takes Elliott home, and everyone gets into BMX – for a few years at least!

The birth of freestyle

Tricks and jumps (freestyle riding) became even more popular than racing. Whether it was showing off between races, or just fooling around in the park, freestyle could be done anywhere! Freestyle contests began to spring up in the early 1980s. Looking back now, these early competitions seem very old fashioned. Today, you would never see anyone in pink leathers hopping around on a day-glo bike!

FOOTPLANT

Early freestylers wore full race gear. Riders found their own style, as Steve Grace demonstrates with a footplant on a mini-ramp (see page 13).

FLATLAND

Flatland (balancing and hopping tricks on a flat surface) soon developed into rolling and scuffing moves such as this locomotive.

Halfpipe and street riding

In the mid 1980s, riders grew more frustrated with organized freestyle contests – they were anything but 'free'. As a result, riders took to the streets, riding whatever obstacles they could. Skateboarding was a major influence. Skaters built the first big halfpipes (see right), which were popular with BMX riders.

HALFPIPES

Two curved walls make up a halfpipe. The walls slope gradually from flat to vertical. The slope, or arc, is called the transition.

To be a young BMX rider in the 1980s was great. Endless days of fun seemed to stretch into the future. But the slump came at the tail-end of the decade, as many decided that riding a kid's 50-cm (20-inch) bike was not a grown-up thing to do.

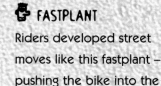

Going underground

In the early 1990s, if you rode a BMX, you were considered a little strange. But despite this alienation, riding progressed much faster than it had during its glory years. Now people rode for the sheer love of it.

Riders began to specialize in one area of riding. While Mat Hoffman and Dennis McCoy pushed ramp riding to the next level, Kevin Jones and Chase Gouin were holed up in a car park for days on end, creating moves that still look good today.

FASTPLANT

Riders developed street moves like this fastplant – pushing the bike into the air with your foot.

ROLLING ON

Flatland evolved with rolling tricks like this bar-split steamroller, done at great speed.

HALFPIPE PROGRESSION

Going through a bike a week was not uncommon for riders such as Carlo Griggs. Here, he kicks his feet into a position called a no-footed candy bar, before re-entering the ramp with his feet back on the pedals.

RIDER-OWNED COMPANIES

Companies like Standard, S&M, Hoffman and 2-Hip, along with now defunct Homeless Bikes, were the first 'rider-owned' companies of the 1990s. Mat Hoffman and Ron Wilkerson (see right) were company founders, as well as contest organizers. Their work with riders such as Joe Johnson and Brian Blyther, one of the smoothest ramp riders ever (see right) helped to shape the sport of BMX as we know it today.

Decent bikes
These days, BMX bikes are generally designed to be strong, but simple.

⚙ FOUNDING FATHERS
From left, Johnson, Hoffman, Wilkerson and Blyther.

⚙ THE CHASM!
Between 1992 and 1997 the Backyard Jams were a sign of the rebirth of BMX. Here, Fuzzy Hall clears the traditional big jump – the 'chasm' in 1992.

Emerging from the gloom

At the start of the 1990s, BMX competitions were low-key affairs. But by 1995, thousands of people were watching riders competing in the Extreme Games. BMX began to return to the public eye, and a whole new breed of riders was enticed into the sport. The Backyard Jam, a contest in a field in Hastings in 1997, attracted around 4000 spectators with minimal advertising. Things were on the up again.

Specialization

In the contests of the 1980s riders were expected to compete in both flatland and ramp disciplines. Often, the best riders did well in both. Dennis McCoy earned his living as a ramp rider, and was once world flatland champion, too.

Dedication

As the sport progressed, it splintered into different disciplines. Many riders dedicated themselves to just one form of riding. This affected the way they rode and their bike set-up. But some riders are more imaginative, and are willing to try their hands at more than one style of riding.

STREET RIDING

Use the world around you to ride how you want – up a tree even.

FLATLAND

Simon O'Brien spins by scuffing the tyre with his foot.

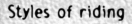

DIRT

This rider is performing a backflip over a large double jump – just one style of dirt riding (see page 16).

Styles of riding

As bike riding has evolved, a few broad styles have emerged. Sometimes the boundaries between these styles have become blurred, depending on what and where you choose to ride. So, pick and mix from ramp, street, flat and dirt.

RAMP RIDING

As this rider shows, you can still have fun with both wheels firmly on the ramp.

Equipment

BMX design has seen many unnecessary gimmicks come and go. Today, you can rely on a bike from a reputable company to do the job and do it well. For the new rider, this means that even a cheap modern bike will outride and outlast a bike that would have cost two or three times more, just a few years ago.

🎃 DIRT BIKE

A dirt bike has no real need for a front brake. The wheel pegs are removed to make the bike lighter.

GUIDE #2

BREAKTHROUGHS IN BIKE DESIGN

Frame gussets These metal plates are welded on to the frame for strength, but they add hardly any weight.

Decent tyres High pressure tyres protect your wheels from dents, and a strong sidewall stops the inner tube escaping.

The Aheadset
The bearings and cups that allow the forks to turn in the frame are known as the headset. The 'Aheadset' design allows the stem that holds the handlebars to fit firmly around the forks, so the inside of the fork tubing can be thick in the right places.

Strong dropouts, socket pegs Dropouts are where the wheels connect with the frame. With pegs, these protect the bike.

Ramp riding

Go to any skatepark and you will see a massive variety of ramps, from full-blown 4-metre (13-foot) halfpipes, through amazing mini-ramps, down to a simple wedge ramp hidden away in the corner. The riding that can be done on these ramps is as varied as the design of the ramps themselves.

WORKING UP

Work on being able to land safely, then try simple airborne tricks, such as this cancan.

INVERT

Carlo Griggs inverts (turns his bike upside down) during an air.

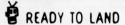

READY TO LAND

Dave Mirra picks his landing spot carefully after a large air.

Vert

Vert riding, on the sheer vertical face of a quarterpipe or halfpipe, is the oldest and most spectacular form of ramp riding. The true experts of the halfpipe have developed their skills with years of practice. They're comfortable performing daring tricks 4 metres (13 feet) above a 4-metre (13-foot) ramp, doing twists and backflips at the same time. Injuries often occur, especially when new tricks are invented – all the top ramp riders bear the scars to prove it!

FULL FACE HELMETS ALL ROUND

Taking one hand and one foot off during an air is called an 'Eddie air'. Full safety equipment is essential for this dangerous trick.

PROGRESSION

Jamie Bestwick performs a turndown air – twisting his handlebars and body into a down-facing position as he reaches the top of the air.

GUIDE #3

MINI-RAMP RIDING

If you don't want to run the risk of performing tricks high above a vert ramp with a sheer vertical slope, mini-ramps are the thing to try. They offer endless trick opportunities, and many riders use mini-ramps to practise grinds (tricks where you scrape part of the bike along, before riding away). Stalls are tricks where you briefly stop the bike before pulling out of the move. These can be performed on the metal coping, or piping, at the edge of the ramp, and along the platform and walls behind the curved transition.

MINI-RAMPS

A mini-ramp is cut off before its slope becomes vertical. This rider is returning backwards, or 'fakie', from a wall behind the mini-ramp.

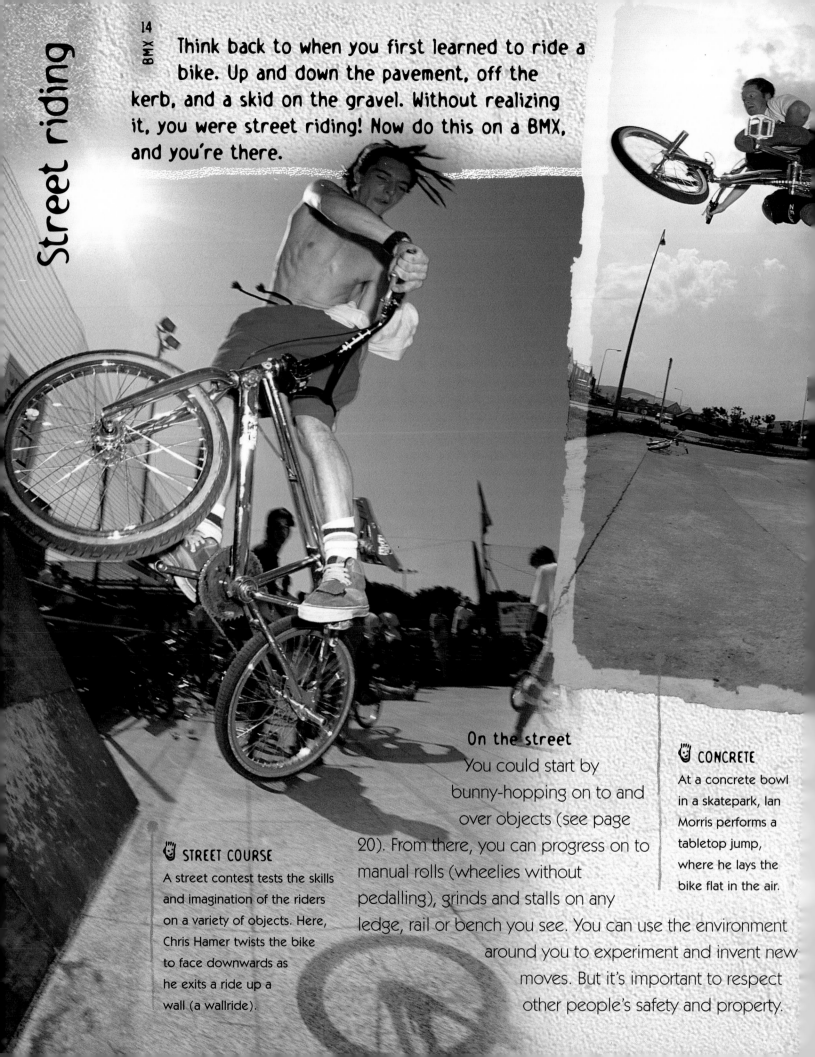

Street riding

Think back to when you first learned to ride a bike. Up and down the pavement, off the kerb, and a skid on the gravel. Without realizing it, you were street riding! Now do this on a BMX, and you're there.

✋ STREET COURSE

A street contest tests the skills and imagination of the riders on a variety of objects. Here, Chris Hamer twists the bike to face downwards as he exits a ride up a wall (a wallride).

On the street

You could start by bunny-hopping on to and over objects (see page 20). From there, you can progress on to manual rolls (wheelies without pedalling), grinds and stalls on any ledge, rail or bench you see. You can use the environment around you to experiment and invent new moves. But it's important to respect other people's safety and property.

✋ CONCRETE

At a concrete bowl in a skatepark, Ian Morris performs a tabletop jump, where he lays the bike flat in the air.

Get off the streets!

In order to reduce the damage and risk caused by street riders and skaters, many local skateparks have been built, based around a 'street course' with large boxes to jump on to and over (jumpboxes), and flat ledges and sloping rails to grind along. These have the advantage of being away from the public, and they are usually well supervised and maintained.

✊ HANDRAIL GRIND
John Taylor grinds backwards down a handrail in Manchester.

REAL STREET vs PARK STREET
Extreme sports programmes on TV often show so-called BMX street contests. You might see a 4-metre-long (13-foot) jumpbox with someone spinning a double backflip high above it. But this sort of trick isn't staged in the street, but in specially-constructed parks. 'True' street riders often dismiss these contests. They feel that their tricks in the real street are every bit as good as the spectacular stunts performed by ramp riders.

Real street?
It would be impossible to perform a trick like this inverted air, just using the obstacles in a real street.

Real street!
For a pure street rider the reward comes from mastering the terrain, not beating the opposition.

Get dirty

If there's one thing every rider wants to do when they first get on a bike, it's to get off the ground. What better way to do that than by aiming yourself at a sculpted pile of dirt?

Racing or jumping?

BMX racing is still at the heart of dirt riding and jumping, and is still going strong today. Racing against seven other riders on a purpose-built track, the aim is to progress through qualifying races into the finals. With jumping, the aim is simple – go as high and as smoothly as you can, perform whatever trick you feel like, and land smoothly. Many people choose to jump because it has less pressure than racing, with an emphasis on personal style rather than straight victory.

🐮 A SPORT FOR ALL

Beginner or expert, male or female, young or old, there will be a race category for you. Stick on a helmet and sign up!

🐮 THE DIRT CIRCUIT

Dirt jumpers aim to get through a set of jumps as smoothly as possible, performing stunts along the way, like this no-footed cancan, with legs kicked out to the side.

3 Berm (banked turn)

1 Starting hill

2 Speed jump

1

2

The trails scene

Trails riders spend as much time digging as they do riding. They're creating huge trails – complex sets of obstacles, which are built purely for jumping over, not for racing through. Trails riders prefer to master their skills alone, rather than perform for a crowd and a panel of judges.

🐮 PRIVATE TRAILS

On private trails, riders can take the time to develop the skills for tricks like this Superman.

GUIDE #5

A BMX TRACK

The ideal BMX track allows speed, passing and big jumps. It should be suitable for riders of all abilities, without being too easy.

4 Doubles

🐮 STAY RELAXED

A calm approach to jumping is needed – fight with your bike in the air and it will look bad, and the landing will be worse. Aim to bring it in smoothly, ready to tackle the next jump.

GUIDE #6

TRICKS OR STYLE?

Is it better to pull off a simple but stylish jump and land as smoothly as ice, or launch into the air, fling the bars around, remove all your limbs, and land like a tonne of bricks? In many dirt jumping contests, this debate can be endless. Do you get through the set of jumps cleanly, or perform some amazing stunt with a heavy landing? Ideally, everyone would like to ride smoothly and cleanly, while also pulling off some tricks – surely the mark of a great rider!

Fast and stylish

Spinning 360 degrees, while spinning the handlebars a full rotation – the truckdriver jump.

Land it!

The tailwhip involves spinning the frame in mid-air, and landing smoothly on the pedals.

Flatland - the purest form?

Flatland is an aspect of freestyle that is often overlooked by many within BMX itself. TV programmes in particular prefer to showcase the more spectacular areas of freestyle. The main reason for this is that flatland is simply very, very difficult!

Dedicated riders

Because there are fewer rewards, flatland has become a closely bonded community of dedicated riders. Originality and style are at the core of flatland. Riders must develop their own tricks and combinations. Imitation is not seen as a form of flattery, but closer to theft! In a contest situation, riders are generally scored on overall impression, and it is often difficult to choose a clear winner. Many flatlanders have chosen to turn their backs on the contest scene, and may ride simply for their own enjoyment. Don't ignore flatland – a few simple tricks can improve your overall bike control, and be turned into a ramp or street move. It's not always important to become a world beater, but it is important to be able to enjoy riding in any form.

FLAT AND DRY

In flat and dry conditions, Lincoln Blacksley jumps to switch his feet around, mid-trick, while spinning on his front wheel.

HUMBLE BEGINNINGS

The headstand was an early, simple balancing trick, which was quickly left behind by more complicated moves.

BRAKES OR NO BRAKES?

The set-up of a flatlander's bike is as individual as his or her style. One of the main, recent developments has been the choice of some riders to remove their brakes, and instead rely on balance and bike control to pull off moves. Naturally this makes many moves harder, and they can look less controlled than when pulled off on a bike with brakes. Many riders think it's unfair to compare riding with brakes with brakeless flatland – they're completely different disciplines.

Brakes

Stephen Green uses his front brake to change direction and position in a front-wheel scuffing trick.

No brakes

With no brakes, Alex Vickers uses his momentum to spin around backwards and in circles.

Getting started

You've read about the history of the sport, watched some videos and tried out a friend's bike. Now you want a piece of the action. Where do you start? First of all, you need to get a bike, and learn to ride it properly.

Get the right bike

The biggest mistake a beginner can make is to buy the wrong bike. It's best to avoid buying a so-called BMX from a catalogue. The chances are it's not really a BMX, but a cheap imitation. A specialist shop will be able to recommend plenty of well-designed, good value bikes, made by famous companies. They can also advise you on the best bikes for your style of riding.

UNFAMILIAR
Its low seat and small wheels will make your BMX feel strange at first.

The bunny-hop

The bunny-hop is the basis of trick BMX riding. It unlocks virtually every trick in the sport. If you learn the bunny-hop, you'll be able to jump higher, get out of the top of ramps, and get into and out of countless street moves.

BUNNY-HOP KEY

1 Approach the object at a reasonable pace.
2 As you near the object pull up the front wheel.
3 Begin to shift your weight forwards.
4 Pull up the back end by tucking your legs up.
5 Pushing forwards on the bars helps straighten the bike in the air.
6 Lower the back end with your legs to bring it in for the landing.

First steps

Now you have your bike, simply ride it, at the park, or anywhere away from traffic. It's important to be confident handling the bike before you move on to harder tricks. Learn to jump and bunny-hop first, then you can progress on to flatland.

🐾 ROCKET JUMP

The near-vertical rocket jump is easily learned, once you can bunny-hop.

EASY DOES IT

Like any extreme sport, BMX riding is harder than it looks. You shouldn't head for the local trails or skatepark on day one. If you get to know your new bike first, you'll be much less likely to have an accident. Your bike will seem uncomfortable and heavy, compared to a normal bicycle. It will also work loose – take it to the bike shop for a 30-day tightening. There are many unwritten rules and ethics, about who can go where and when on the track. It's a good idea to visit without your bike to find out about these. Skateparks have experienced staff who are there to help. Don't be afraid to ask!

GUIDE #8

THE DECADE

1 Roll forwards slowly. Pull on both brakes, trying to do a small 'endo', where the back wheel leaves the ground. Rock back on to the back wheel and pull up the front end. 2 Kick off the seatpost. 3 Jump around the headtube (the top of the bike), keeping your arms locked. 4 Land with your other foot on the seatpost. 5 Bring your foot on to the pedal. 6 & 7 Release your brakes and ride out.

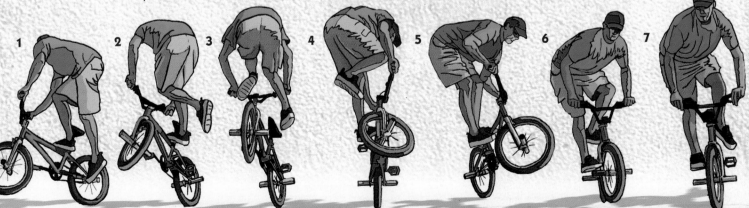

Getting better

Once you get a bit of control and confidence, and learn a few tricks, it's time to find somewhere to show off your new skills. The best places are public skateparks, or tracks with a few jumps.

Work out your style

Once you find a ramp or a jump, spend a bit of time working out which way you turn, and which foot you lead with. This should feel natural, like being left or right handed. Now seek out a bigger skatepark – BMX and skateboarding magazines have park directories.

WALLRIDE

The aim of a wallride is to ride along the wall before jumping back on to the ramp.

Social life

Bigger parks will benefit from being supervised, with a good variety of ramps. The best ones are indoors, so you can ride them all year round. You'll also be able to meet other riders, and discuss new ideas and moves. Meeting riders at parks should also open up other opportunities, to find out about trails, street riding areas, and the chance to travel to jams or contests.

KEEP WATCHING

If you get into flatland, contests can be good places to find a few more people to ride with. You'll be able to watch experienced riders tackling complicated rolling tricks, like this hitchhiker.

GUIDE #9

TRICKS TO TAKE YOU FURTHER

360 jump

Learn this trick on the ground first. Twist your body, and the bike will follow. The speed you need to twist depends on the distance you jump. Start off with small jumps, then move on to proper jumps. Gradually, you can increase the time you're in the air.

Float it A 360 should be floated, not forced, over a jump, with the rotation ending as you bring it in for landing.

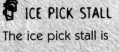

HEAD UP

This rider is midway through a 360 jump. Note how he is checking ahead where his landing will be.

Busdriver

Jump, pinch the seat with your knees, spin the bars, catch the bars, land. This trick isn't easy at first. Always wear a helmet, and expect to fall off. Practise barspins on the ground first – roll slowly, and just lean back a little and spin.

NOT TOO EARLY

This rider starts his busdriver when he is fully in the air – spin the bars too early and it will affect your jump badly.

ICE PICK STALL

The ice pick stall is when you stall on the back peg.

Grinds and stalls

Stick some pegs on your bike and try a few stalls on a ramp or ledge. If you stall on your front peg, that's a toothpick. The nosepick is a front wheel stall. Try some grinds along the coping of ramps, or along concrete ledges. These tricks will tell you if your bike is up to the job, and whether you need to save up to buy some new parts!

1

2

3

4

5

One thing you will soon discover when you take up BMX is that a large part of your time is spent rolling around on the floor. No matter what area of BMX you choose, falling off and injuries are part of the package.

Pain is temporary – glory is forever

Fearless riders

One look at the crash section of a video will tell you that few tricks are pulled off first time. The risk of injuries can be minimized through riding realistically. It takes many hours in the saddle to learn what needs to be done in some moves. Learning to fall properly can mean sliding on to kneepads, throwing a bike away, or running out of a jump – none of these things comes naturally!

🕹 PAYING THE PRICE

Even when fully protected, injuries happen. Here, Dave Mirra dons an ice pack between runs to calm another ache.

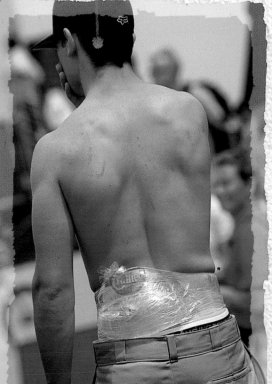

Knee pads
Hard caps help you to slide out of tricks – if you have time!

Gloves
Minor handscrapes can stop you riding, but are easily preventable.

What to wear?

Choosing the right safety gear for a ride is fairly obvious. You don't need to dress up like a vert rider if you're riding to the shops. It's quite easy to remain well protected, but still look normal, as the safety gear on this page shows. The golden rule is to ride sensibly and appreciate the risks.

Helmet
A helmet can be weakened by a heavy blow, and should be replaced.

FASHION?

Vans These shoes were a huge hit.

Don't be put off by someone laughing at your 'unfashionable' bike. It is still a BMX. Trends in bike set-ups come and go, so try to set up your bike so you feel comfortable with it, then work out your own riding style. Just be thankful you missed out on some of the early BMX fashions. Fortunately, dayglo uniforms, big goggles and wafer thin shoes are no longer standard gear.

Checked trousers Happily, these are also a thing of the past.

Knee/shin combos
These might not look great, but they can save you from a great deal of pain.

The money moves

The sequences on these pages are the real milestone tricks in freestyle - the ones that pushed riding to another level. You may be surprised to learn just how old some of these tricks are.

 900 AIR

An unbelievable amount of rotation is needed to rotate 900 degrees. This is Simon Tabron in mid-rotation.

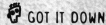

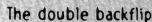

The flair

A flair is a backflip with a 180 degree turn added, allowing the rider to re-enter forwards. Back in 1990, Mat Hoffman performed a backflip fakie on a halfpipe – he went straight up the ramp, flipped in the air and landed backwards. The freestyle world was amazed. Before anyone could even think about copying it, Mat popped up three months later in Mansfield, England, and pulled out a flair 2 metres (7 feet) out of the ramp, on only his second attempt.

GOT IT DOWN

Dave Mirra was one of the first to perfect the flair's technique, pulling it at will.

The double backflip

A real contest winner – it takes a lot of time in the air to fit in the rotations. In the early 1990s, it took a particular type of rider to go for this. Bob Kohl, a Chicago stuntman, went for a couple in 1992 without much success. Up stepped Jay Miron, nicknamed the Canadian Beast, who makes his living as a rider and as the owner of MacNeil bikes. Finding a jump big enough to allow all those rotations took a while. After a couple of trips to casualty, Jay pulled the trick off in front of a live TV audience in 1996.

The 900 degree aerial

When you're riding a vert ramp with sheer vertical sides, the idea of throwing in two and a half rotations high above the coping seems a bit far fetched. Not to Mike Dominguez, a top rider of the 1980s. As far back as late 1986, Dominguez was throwing himself around 900 degrees, but he only succeeded a few times, mostly on his own ramp in private. It wasn't until 1989 that Mat Hoffman pulled this off in competition. It was only his second attempt, and he had a broken thumb. Today the 900 is still a fairly rare sight, with Hoffman himself and Simon Tabron being the main riders to achieve it regularly.

If the sequence doesn't make any sense it's because a three-sixty backflip doesn't make any sense. From here on in let this be known as a Zak Flip.

DiG CENTRE-PARTING

💀 THE $20,000 FLIP

Steven Murray unleashed his first double flips at the 2001 X-Games. He took away the first place prize of $20,000.

💀 360 BACKFLIP

Zach Shaw added a 360 degree turn to a backflip jump. The 'Zachflip' was born, and riders are still trying to work out how to do one, even today!

Masters of their sport

These riders have taken BMX to new extremes. Bravery, imagination, dedication and years of practice have taken them to the very top of their sport.

Mat Hoffman

If there is one rider who has pushed the sport of BMX further than anyone else, it has to be Mat.

THE CHAMP
Mat Hoffman with the winner's trophy at a competition in Paris.

A regular on TV and videogames, Mat is the most innovative halfpipe rider of all time. He has invented countless variations and experiments at the limits of ramp riding. Mat has devoted himself completely to riding, running contest series and the Hoffman bike company. His numerous injuries prove his commitment to the sport.

Martti Kuoppa

Martti is an incredible flatland rider from Helsinki, Finland. He first appeared on the worldwide scene at the world championships in 1997, riding with his own distinctive style. This style, and those of other riders such as Viki Gomez and Phil Dolan, signalled the beginning of a European force that was pushing out the North Americans at the top of flatland's ranks. Martti has won countless contests, riding with superhuman speed and fluidity, as he links impossible-looking tricks together in one smooth motion.

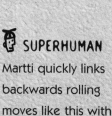

SUPERHUMAN
Martti quickly links backwards rolling moves like this with other hard tricks.

Dave Mirra

Hailing from North Carolina on the East coast of the USA, Dave is another household name in BMX. He has won more big vert and street contests than any other rider, with ten X-Games gold medals to his name. He is capable of riding in virtually every discipline.

 **THE MIRACLE BOY**

Dave Mirra demonstrates a busdriver trick from a halfpipe.

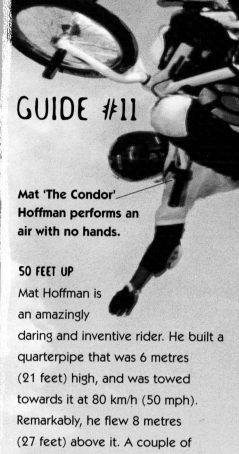

GUIDE #11

Mat 'The Condor' Hoffman performs an air with no hands.

50 FEET UP

Mat Hoffman is an amazingly daring and inventive rider. He built a quarterpipe that was 6 metres (21 feet) high, and was towed towards it at 80 km/h (50 mph). Remarkably, he flew 8 metres (27 feet) above it. A couple of experiments and a serious injury followed, with a few years away. In 2000, Mat was back on the case – a 7.5-metre (25-foot) ramp, an 8.5-metre (28-foot) air, and a crushed helmet. Not for the faint-hearted!

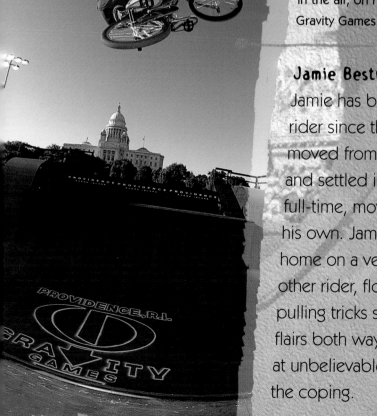

LONG WAY DOWN

Jamie Bestwick spins 540 degrees, high in the air, on his way to first place in the Gravity Games contest.

Jamie Bestwick

Jamie has been a top vert rider since the early 1990s. He moved from Derby, England, and settled in the USA to ride full-time, moving into a class of his own. Jamie is more at home on a vert ramp than any other rider, flowing endlessly, pulling tricks such as 540s and flairs both ways, while keeping at unbelievable heights above the coping.

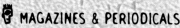

Useful information

BMX

Once BMX gets a grip on you, it's hard to let go. What was once just a sport for the kids now involves people aged from 4 to 40, all of whom have been bitten by the bug. To get started on the right tracks, it's important to get the right information.

MAGAZINES & PERIODICALS

Dig BMX Magazine

A bi-monthly publication based in Belfast, mostly covering the British and US scenes, with some European content too. The BMX lifestyle and image is central to *Dig*, with much thought going into the photography, writing and layout.

Ride (UK) BMX Magazine

Published nine times a year, *Ride* mostly aims to cover all aspects of the British scene, and it succeeds. With full coverage of contests big and small, an in-depth news section, and unbiased bike and frame tests, *Ride* will help you get up to speed with what's happening.

Fat Magazine

What started as a photocopied fanzine is now a huge internet magazine, covering the world scene from its base in Holland. Log on to www.fatbmx.com for news, gossip, and the most in-depth events calendar available.

Also available:

Dirt – a UK magazine that includes race and trails coverage; *BMX Rider* – a recent UK publication; *Ride* (US), *Transworld BMX* and *BMX Plus* are US based magazines often available in the UK.

PLACES TO RIDE

There is an ever-growing number of ramp parks. Both *Dig* and *Ride* magazines publish updated park directories in each issue, listing facilities, phone numbers and addresses. Your safest bet is to consult one of these.

NATIONAL EVENTS

The British Cycling Federation runs a national series of BMX races around the country – see the website (www.bcf.uk.com) for details.

With no national freestyle organizations, most contests and jams are organized on an informal basis. Keep an eye on websites and in the magazines for dates of events near you. Look out for the Backyard Jams, the Urban Games, the Bike Show, Level Vibes flatland contests, Lord street jams, and SK8 and Ride skatepark jams, all of which run regularly each year.

USEFUL WEBSITES

www.digbmx.com – the site for *Dig* magazine, with subscription deals, and an interactive skatepark directory.

www.ridebmxmagazine.co.uk – the site for *Ride UK* magazine, includes a very useful database with all recent bike tests, which should include the bike that interests you.

www.ride4life.co.uk – an independent racing website with links to regional race organizations.

www.theflatlander.com – the main source of information for the flatland world.

All the Internet addresses (URLs) given in this book were valid at the time of going to press. However, due to the dynamic nature of the Internet, some addresses may have changed, or sites may have ceased to exist since publication. While the author and publishers regret any inconvenience this may cause readers, no responsibility for any such changes can be accepted by either the author or the publishers.

Glossary

aerial

trick done in the air, not on the ground

fakie

backwards

flip

spin over in the air backwards or forwards

forks

parts of the frame that attach to the wheels

frame

main part of the bike, on to which wheels and saddle fit

grind

any trick where a part of the bike such as the pegs or chain scrapes (grinds) along before riding away. Examples include double peg grinds, ice pick grinds and feeble grinds. They can be performed on ramps, ledges, benches and rails.

gusset

tube or plate welded on to the frame to add strength. They are usually found behind the headtube and bottom bracket.

halfpipe

ramp with curved sides that looks like a pipe cut in half

motocross

motorcycle racing over rough terrain

180

half turn, landing backwards. If a move is named after a number, like a 180, 360, 540 or 900, the number refers to the degrees of rotation that the bike goes through.

pegs

short tubes of hard metal that fit either side of the wheels on some BMX bikes. The pegs can be used for grinding and stalling, or you can balance on the bike, standing on the pegs.

quarterpipe

ramp that is half the size of a halfpipe

stall

trick that involves momentarily stopping before pulling out of the move. Stalls are performed on the coping of a ramp, a rail, or a ledge. Examples are abubacas, nosepicks and fufanus.

trails

complex sets of jumps built just for jumping, instead of racing

transition

curved part of a ramp. A 7.5-metre (25-foot) transition ramp has a curve with a radius of 7.5 metres (25 feet).

wheelie

lifting the front wheel off the ground and cycling along on the rear wheel

Index